The Li

of Quotations on

Sustainable Business

By Wayne Visser

Paperback edition published in 2017
by Kaleidoscope Futures, London, UK.

Cover photography and design by Wayne Visser.

Printing and distribution by Lulu.com.

ISBN 978-1-908875-39-6

Non-fiction Books by Wayne Visser

Beyond Reasonable Greed: Why Sustainable Business is a Much Better Idea!

South Africa: Reasons to Believe

Corporate Citizenship in Africa: Lessons from the Past, Paths to the Future

Business Frontiers: Social Responsibility, Sustainable Development and Economic Justice

The A to Z of Corporate Social Responsibility: A Complete Reference Guide to Concepts, Codes and Organisations

Making A Difference: Purpose-Inspired Leadership for Corporate Sustainability & Responsibility

Landmarks for Sustainability

The Top 50 Sustainability Books

The World Guide to CSR: A Country by Country Analysis of Corporate Sustainability and Responsibility

The Age of Responsibility: CSR 2.0 and the New DNA of Business

The Quest for Sustainable Business: An Epic Journey in Search of Corporate Responsibility

Corporate Sustainability & Responsibility: An Introductory Text on CSR Theory & Practice – Past, Present & Future

CSR 2.0: Transforming Corporate Sustainability and Responsibility

Disrupting the Future: Great Ideas for Creating a Much Better World

This is Tomorrow: Artists for a Sustainable Future

Sustainable Frontiers: Unlocking Change Through Business, Leadership and Innovation

The CSR International Research Compendium: Volumes 1-3

The World Guide to Sustainable Enterprise: Volumes 1-4

The Little Book of Quotations on Social Responsibility

The Little Book of Quotations on Sustainable Business

Fiction Books by Wayne Visser

About the Author

Dr Wayne Visser is Professor of Integrated Value and holds the Chair in Sustainable Transformation at Antwerp Management School. He is Director of the think-tank and media company, Kaleidoscope Futures and Fellow at Cambridge University's Institute for Sustainability Leadership. His work as a strategy analyst, sustainability advisor, CSR expert, futurist and professional speaker has taken him to over 70 countries in the past 20 years. Dr Visser is author of 28 books – including *Sustainable Frontiers: Unlocking Change Through Business, Leadership and Innovation*. Dr Visser has been recognised as a top 100 thought-leader in trustworthy business and received the Global CSR Excellence & Leadership Award. He founded CSR International, after obtaining a PhD in corporate social responsibility. He previously served as Director of Sustainability Services for KPMG and Strategy Analyst for Capgemini in South Africa. Dr Visser lives in Cambridge, UK.

Website: www.waynevisser.com

Email: wayne@waynevisser.com

"Sustainability is a new way of perceiving business - its purpose, its methods and its impacts"

From: Beyond Reasonable Greed

"We all have footprints.
But we can lighten the
tread and ensure they are
heading in a more
sustainable direction"

From: Sustainable Frontiers

"Sustainability issues
give us the opportunity
to create meaning
at a personal level"

From: Making a Difference

"In our modern
economies and businesses,
unlimited growth is
constantly striven for,
institutionalised,
almost idolised"

From: Business Frontiers

"When it comes to sustainability, we are actually talking about changing a vastly complex system"

From: Sustainable Frontiers

"Eco-subsidies are a way to internalize the externalities that the market fails to take account of"

From: The A to Z of Corporate Social Responsibility

"To succeed, sustainability has to be translated into the language of the business or sector or functional area"

From: *Sustainable Frontiers*

"As our knowledge of the
state of the planet has
improved, denial is no
longer a credible position"

From: Landmarks for Sustainability

"The land is not

there to serve us,

but we need to live

in community

with the land"

From: The Top 50 Sustainability Books

"At the macro level, almost every indicator of our social, environmental and ethical health is in decline"

From: The Age of Responsibility

"Sustainability reports are practically burping with all the 'low hanging fruit' companies have gorged on"

From: Sustainable Frontiers

"International regulatory frameworks are absolutely essential in trying to halt the sixth mass extinction"

From: The Quest for Sustainable Business

"Can we really afford
to talk about long-term
sustainability, when
short-term survival
is so hard to achieve?"

From: Disrupting the Future

"For companies that can adapt and respond to sustainability, there are new markets to capture and profits to be made"

From: Beyond Reasonable Greed

"Unless sustainability is
built into the company's
compensation schemes,
middle managers
will not align"

From: Sustainable Frontiers

"The circular economy -
where closed-loop
production brings us
closer to zero waste - is a
real business opportunity"

From: Sustainable Frontiers

"Existential striving is
closely associated with
the nature of work
in sustainability"

From: Making a Difference

"In nature, unlimited
physical growth is almost
nowhere to be seen;
when it does occur,
we call it cancer"

From: Business Frontiers

"Sadly, many government subsidies currently support ecologically harmful and unsustainable practices"

From: The A to Z of Corporate Social Responsibility

"Sustainability must
be recast as being
fundamentally about
the way a company
does business"

From: Sustainable Frontiers

"We now have evidence
of the scale of our human
impacts, the seriousness
of our predicament and
the urgency for action"

From: Landmarks for Sustainability

"Community without
land is empty, so by
threatening the land
we are threatening
community"

From: The Top 50 Sustainability Books

"What many people

fail to appreciate

is how uneconomic

our environmental

destruction really is"

From: The Age of Responsibility

"Most people in most
parts of the world don't
believe a sustainable
future is necessarily
a better future"

From: Sustainable Frontiers

"When we have no personal experience of wilderness, do we lose our ability to care deeply about nature?"

From: The Quest for Sustainable Business

"The sobering fact is that we face a future in which saving the world may have to wait, while we save ourselves first"

From: Disrupting the Future

"To survive in the sustainability era, companies will have to move beyond their aggressive tendencies"

From: Sustainable Frontiers

"For companies
ill-prepared, sustainability
is going to become a
financial burden; even a
threat to survival"

From: Beyond Reasonable Greed

"Unless the world's booming economies can lighten the weighty anchor of resource consumption, we will all sink"

From: Sustainable Frontiers

"Corporate sustainability
is a values-laden umbrella
for the interface between
business, society and
the environment"

From: Making a Difference

"What happens in nature
is that quantitative growth
is always superseded by
qualitative growth"

From: Business Frontiers

"By incorporating social
and environmental costs,
the market is able to work
efficiently to bring about
sustainable outcomes"

From: The A to Z of Corporate Social Responsibility

"Good performance on independent sustainability ratings is one way to counter low levels of trust in business"

From: Sustainable Frontiers

"We are substantially
diminishing the benefits
that future generations
will be able to obtain
from ecosystems"

From: Landmarks for Sustainability

"The land, the people and the other species are all part of a circular system, which humans have disconnected from"

From: The Top 50 Sustainability Books

"Growth and
development move in
parallel up to a threshold
point, after which quality
of life is eroded due to
externalities"

From: The Quest for Sustainable Business

"To make real progress towards sustainability, companies must first admit that we face a serious global crisis"

From: Beyond Reasonable Greed

"Customers and
governments need to
give up their compulsive
throw-away habits
and embrace the
take-back economy"

From: Sustainable Frontiers

"Environmental champions imbue a range of characteristics, including catalyst, sponsor, facilitator and demonstrator"

From: Making a Difference

"A growing economy
is getting bigger;
a developing economy
is getting better"

From: Business Frontiers

"The bottom line is that we are gambling with our climate future, but we can still spread our bets"

From: Sustainable Frontiers

"We must accept that,
in the case of public goods
(like clean air, water and
a healthy environment),
markets tend to fail"

From: The A to Z of Corporate Social Responsibility

"We desperately need more Apollo-like sustainability missions that the public can get genuinely excited about"

From: Sustainable Frontiers

"If we fail to reconnect with nature, nature will suffer and humanity will suffer"

From: The Top 50 Sustainability Books

"We must be honest
about the social and
environmental costs
of growth: the world
is getting more unequal
and unsustainable"

From: The Quest for Sustainable Business

"The fact of the matter
is that our lifestyles,
our products and
our business processes
are unsustainable"

From: Beyond Reasonable Greed

"The proliferation of
sustainability standards
has led to market
confusion for investors
and consumers"

From: Sustainable Frontiers

"Sustainability can become a deeply personal quest for meaning in life and work"

From: Making a Difference

"At one level
sustainability is
simply about the ability
to survive (and thrive)
over the long term"

From: The A to Z of Corporate Social Responsibility

"Land is a system of

interdependent parts,

best regarded

as a community,

not a commodity"

From: The Top 50 Sustainability Books

"We need a qualitatively different kind of growth, redesigned to have zero or even positive environmental impacts"

From: The Quest for Sustainable Business

"Sustainability stands on the brink of transforming the underlying business model of the past few hundred years"

From: Beyond Reasonable Greed

"What is missing across
the sustainability
standards arena is
greater clarity and
more co-ordination"

From: Sustainable Frontiers

"Sustainability managers are motivated by making a difference through the positive impact of their work on society"

From: Making a Difference

"There are deep psychological - even existential - reasons why we 'do' sustainability"

From: Sustainable Frontiers

"Sustainability is seldom an objective, scientific or neutral concept, and more often a normative or subjective topic"

From: The A to Z of Corporate Social Responsibility

"We can understand
and appreciate our
place in nature only
by understanding
nature as a whole"

From: The Top 50 Sustainability Books

"Sustainability reporting
has distracted us from
a far more important
trend, namely social
and environmental
accounting"

From: The Quest for Sustainable Business

"The old ways of the past are no longer appropriate for a post-industrial, sustainability-driven society"

From: Beyond Reasonable Greed

"Sustainability reporting
is only one face of
the transparency coin;
on the other side is
sustainability ratings"

From: Sustainable Frontiers

"Sustainability catalysts
get meaning from
initiating change, giving
strategic direction and
influencing leadership"

From: Making a Difference

"Our duty is to preserve the integrity, stability and beauty of the biotic community"

From: The Top 50 Sustainability Books

"Sustainability is not only a new scientific concept; it is an entirely new business philosophy based on a new mythology"

From: Beyond Reasonable Greed

"Standardization, comparability and consistency in sustainability ratings are urgently required"

From: Sustainable Frontiers

"Sustainability activists'
purpose comes from
fighting for a just cause
and leaving a legacy of
an improved society"

From: Making a Difference

"Land is a community
of living things.
This calls for the
study of ecology"

From: The Top 50 Sustainability Books

"Sustainability requires
that business thinks
differently about its role in
society and how it goes
about what it does"

From: Beyond Reasonable Greed

"New social technologies promise (or threaten) to transform sustainability reporting. Broadcast is out; dialogue is in."

From: Sustainable Frontiers

"Human beings are not
in control of nature.
Our survival depends
on the health of all
in the web of life"

From: The Top 50 Sustainability Books

"Sustainability only works
when it is a passionately
embraced philosophy that
infuses every business
level and action"

From: Beyond Reasonable Greed

"So much of making a successful transition to a more sustainable future depends on letting go"

From: Sustainable Frontiers

"Spaceship Earth is a metaphor for understanding the planet as a closed system; hence, there is no 'away'"

From: The Top 50 Sustainability Books

"In a sustainability era,
a company's success will
depend on cultivating
multi-stakeholder,
win-win relationships"

From: Beyond Reasonable Greed

"If we are to reach sustainable frontiers, it must begin with changing our collective minds"

From: Sustainable Frontiers

"Humanity must learn how to survive and thrive using only the sun's regenerative energy and their own intellectual abilities"

From: The Top 50 Sustainability Books

"Like Dumbo,
sustainable companies
need to believe they can
fly against the odds and
in the face of public
perception"

From: Beyond Reasonable Greed

"Sustainability, I've discovered to be many things, but not an effective strategy for change – at least, not yet"

From: Sustainable Frontiers

"A precondition of a sustainable world is that population and capital growth need to be stabilized"

From: The Top 50 Sustainability Books

"Business and economic growth will always be dumb - rather than smart - until it mimics the intelligence of ecosystems"

From: Beyond Reasonable Greed

"The essential idea of sustainability is about as exciting as watching lettuce wilt under the midday sun"

From: Sustainable Frontiers

"There are two ways out
of ecological overshoot:
a well-organised retraction
to sustainable levels, or a
nature-induced collapse"

From: The Top 50 Sustainability Books

"Sustainability raises
the bar of legislation;
so sustainable companies
proactively anticipate
the rising tide"

From: Beyond Reasonable Greed

"Sustainability has won
many battles, but has lost
the war for the hearts and
minds of the people"

From: Sustainable Frontiers

"Unsustainable companies will increasingly incur fines, penalties and clean-up costs and be targeted for litigation"

From: Beyond Reasonable Greed

"Sustainability has been warning of scarcity and survival, when what people want is prosperity and thriving"

From: Sustainable Frontiers

"As the rules of trade shift, sustainable companies will increasingly refuse to trade with predatory companies"

From: Beyond Reasonable Greed

"The sustainability
movement has failed to
understand what it means
to be human"

From: Sustainable Frontiers

"In the future, access to finance by unsustainable companies will become more difficult and expensive"

From: Beyond Reasonable Greed

"Sustainability 'wonks'
believe that they are all
about Progress with a
capital 'P'. The world
remains unconvinced"

From: Sustainable Frontiers

"Avoiding the costs of social and environmental impacts will make sustainable companies more profitable in future"

From: Beyond Reasonable Greed

"Sustainability is like a geeky, pimply teenager who has come to our party and turned off the music"

From: Sustainable Frontiers

"The switch to a sustainable economy is creating new market opportunities that smart companies are investing in"

From: Beyond Reasonable Greed

"Sustainability folks keep telling us that we would really be much happier if we stopped having so much darn fun!"

From: Sustainable Frontiers

"Unsustainable companies will increasingly fail the corporate governance acid test applied by investors"

From: Beyond Reasonable Greed

"The key to having a
good time, declares the
sustainability mantra,
is to practice a lot more
self-restraint"

From: Sustainable Frontiers

"It takes a complex mix of different players to bring about lasting change for sustainability"

From: Making a Difference

"Unsustainable companies must expect to suffer consumer boycotts, civil lawsuits and disruptive NGO activism"

From: Beyond Reasonable Greed

"All those on board the sustainability austerity train, say "Hell, yeah!" … What, no one?"

From: Sustainable Frontiers

"Only when sustainability
is an investment criteria
will sustainable companies
will reap fair financial
rewards"

From: Beyond Reasonable Greed

"Sustainability is a bit like chess - it is complex, dynamic and challenging, like an earth-puzzle that needs solving"

From: Sustainable Frontiers

www.ingramcontent.com/pod-product-compliance
Lightning Source LLC
Chambersburg PA
CBHW060626210326
41520CB00010B/1492